A sign with tips for keeping water clean stands in front of the Chua-Chua Botanical Gardens in Farmer Tantoh's hometown of Nkambe, Cameroon.

A road that leads to Akweto, Cameroon, provides a view of the landscape during the dry season.

For small-scale farmers and grassroots environmentalists everywhere —B.P.

For eco-minded people, especially Carol Hinz —M.P.

For people working to better our world, one person at a time —E.Z.

The authors would like to acknowledge Farmer Tantoh Nforba Dieudonne, Mbunkur Quinta Musah, and their respective families for their help and hospitality while researching this book. They would also like to recognize Nfor Kenneth Yinkfu, Fombe Nfor Celestine, Justice Mrs. Grace Kinyang Mabu, Dr. Peter Mabu Tata and family, and Save Your Future Association for supporting us and Tantoh. Your contributions, great and small, will encourage young readers around the world to become stewards for the earth and leaders in their own communities.

Millbrook Press
A division of Lerner Publishing Group, Inc.
241 First Avenue North
Minneapolis, MN 55401 USA

For reading levels and more information, look up this title at www.lernerbooks.com.

All photographs on endpapers courtesy of Baptiste Paul and Miranda Paul.
Map © Laura Westlund/Independent Picture Service.

Designed by Emily Harris.
Main body text set in Stone Informal ITC Std 16/23.
Typeface provided by International Typeface Corporation.
The illustrations in this book were created with cut paper collage, watercolor, pen drawing, and pasted colored pencil.

Library of Congress Cataloging-in-Publication Data

Names: Paul, Baptiste, author. | Paul, Miranda, author. | Zunon, Elizabeth, illustrator.
Title: I am farmer : growing an environmental movement in Cameroon / by Baptiste and Miranda
    Paul ; illustrated by Elizabeth Zunon.
Description: Minneapolis, MN : Millbrook Press, [2019].
Identifiers: LCCN 2018035853 (print) | LCCN 2018039692 (ebook) | ISBN 9781541543805 (eb pdf) |
    ISBN 9781512449143 (lb : alk. paper)
Subjects: LCSH: Agriculture—Cameroon—Juvenile literature. | Environmentalism—Cameroon—
    Juvenile literature.
Classification: LCC S473.C17 (ebook) | LCC S473.C17 P38 2019 (print) | DDC 338.1096711—dc23

LC record available at https://lccn.loc.gov/2018035853

Manufactured in the United States of America
1-42846-26510-7/31/2018

I AM FARMER

GROWING AN ENVIRONMENTAL MOVEMENT IN CAMEROON

BAPTISTE PAUL AND **MIRANDA PAUL**

ILLUSTRATIONS BY
ELIZABETH ZUNON

M MILLBROOK PRESS • MINNEAPOLIS

THIS IS NORTHWESTERN CAMEROON.

Green.

Wet.

Alive.

The rainy season has begun.

A young boy arrives at his grandmother's farm. His feet squish between rows of cabbage and beans. His small hands plunge into the dirt. *"Nshee!"*

"Oh, Tantoh!" His father laughs. His grandmother laughs, too.

They do not stop him.

They understand his joy.

Tantoh rummages through Grandmother's
market basket. A sharp smell fills the air. "Onions!"
He wonders if he can grow them by himself. He
sneaks them under a banana tree.

Each day when he checks on his secret garden, the greens have shriveled a bit more. Eventually, the bulbs dry up.

"Why won't they grow, *ma kfu*?" he asks his grandmother.

"They need sunlight and earth," she says, "and most importantly, water." She explains that nature has its own ways of working.

Tantoh wants to learn more. He wants to learn *everything*.

When he begins school, Tantoh drinks up facts and figures faster than his teacher can pour them onto the chalkboard. His hand shoots up like a cornstalk.

Teachers frown. "Too many questions!"
Students giggle. "What's so interesting about plants and dirt and weather?"

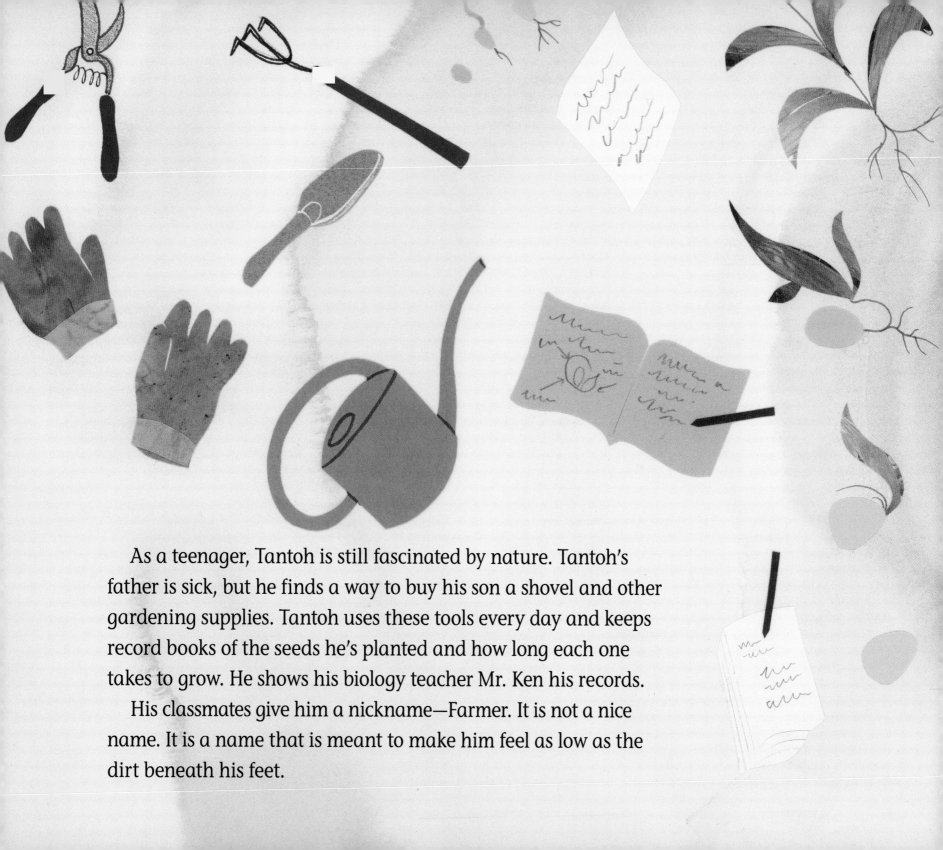

As a teenager, Tantoh is still fascinated by nature. Tantoh's father is sick, but he finds a way to buy his son a shovel and other gardening supplies. Tantoh uses these tools every day and keeps record books of the seeds he's planted and how long each one takes to grow. He shows his biology teacher Mr. Ken his records.

His classmates give him a nickname—Farmer. It is not a nice name. It is a name that is meant to make him feel as low as the dirt beneath his feet.

But Tantoh loves the dirt.
He loves the texture of roots.
He loves the smell of dark, wet soil.
He loves the corn it can grow and the
fufu it provides for his brothers and sisters.
Especially now that his father is dying.

One morning, he makes
himself a new school uniform.
He puts big letters on the front:

Tantoh wears the shirt to school for the rest of high school. His elder brother shakes his head.

"Farmers are very poor." His brother urges him to do well on a special upcoming exam so he can provide for the family. "If you get good marks, you can work in an office. Be a police officer or a teacher."

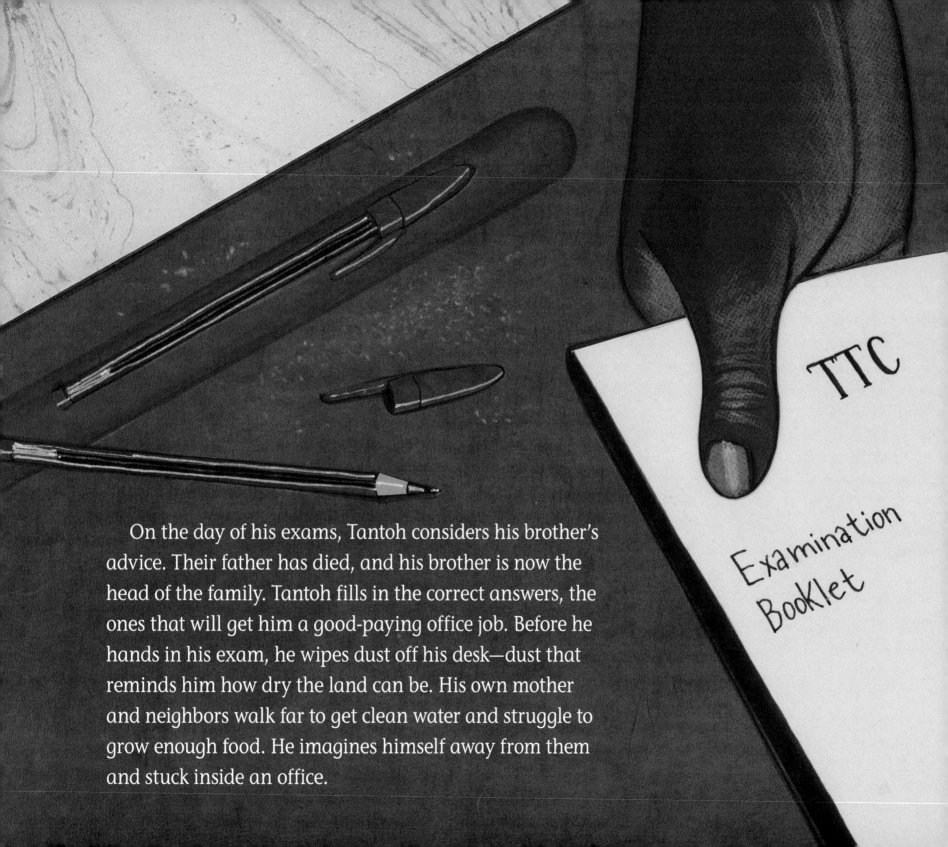

On the day of his exams, Tantoh considers his brother's advice. Their father has died, and his brother is now the head of the family. Tantoh fills in the correct answers, the ones that will get him a good-paying office job. Before he hands in his exam, he wipes dust off his desk—dust that reminds him how dry the land can be. His own mother and neighbors walk far to get clean water and struggle to grow enough food. He imagines himself away from them and stuck inside an office.

He crosses out his answers and hands in his paper.
He signs it, *F*—for Farmer.
His teacher returns it, *F*—for FAIL.

Name: Fe.

Grade: F

Answer 1:

example:

His days at school are over, so the land in his village of Nkambe becomes his classroom. He spends his days (and sometimes nights) digging, planting, reading, asking. Even Mr. Ken, who lives nearby, can't answer all of Farmer Tantoh's questions.

As he works, Farmer Tantoh meets others who share his love for the land and water. One of the people he meets recognizes how important his love of farming is and provides money to send him to college. Tantoh will be able to study the environment and agriculture at a local school. Finally, his classmates and teachers will praise him for talking about the weather, learning about water, and playing with the soil!

At college, Farmer Tantoh is thirsty to learn everything he can. Although he soaks up plenty of facts and figures, clean water is still scarce. He contracts typhoid from drinking the local water. He is so sick, he worries he may not live long enough to graduate.

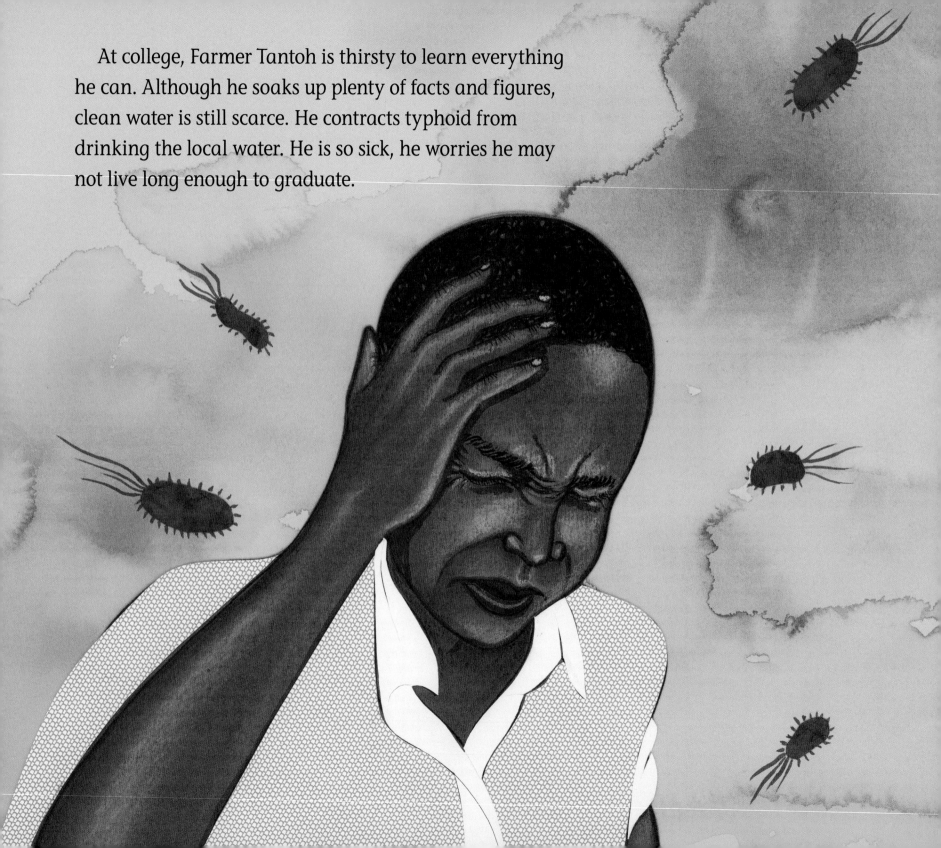

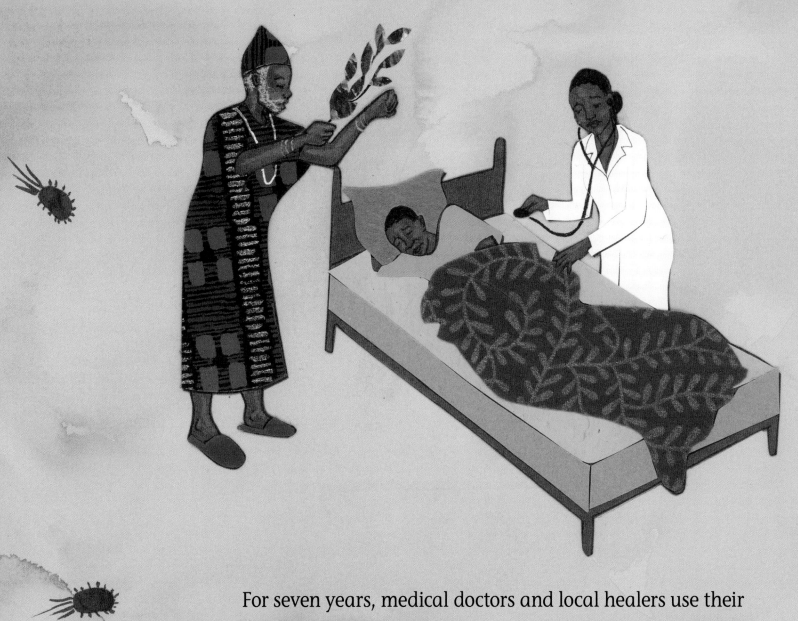

For seven years, medical doctors and local healers use their knowledge, medicines, and herbs to make Farmer Tantoh feel better. During his recovery, he thinks a lot about his future, and the future of his fellow Cameroonians. No one should die from drinking something that is necessary for life: water.

After he is better, Farmer Tantoh gets a chance to continue his studies in the United States. There, he finds out about new ways to save the rain, find clean underground water, and grow gardens and crops without poisoning the soil and wells.

Back in Cameroon, Farmer Tantoh is eager to use what he has learned. People are still getting sick because they don't have clean water. And when the dry season comes, there is hunger and drought. How can he help his people? Resources are limited. Most villages don't have tractors, motorized tillers, or irrigation systems to bring water to fields. Some don't even have roads.

Farmer Tantoh creates a motto to help motivate himself and others: "When you don't have what you want, use what you have." While he doesn't have much, he does have people! Tantoh gathers children and teenagers to join him in the fields. Some laugh at him or shake their heads, but others grab a shovel or hoe.

Together they build botanical gardens and rain gardens that will hold water in the soil. These areas produce food or flowers all year long and provide green spaces to reconnect people with nature. The mayor of his home village, Nkambe, is impressed. Eventually, the mayor promises to make sure the garden stays beautiful for years to come. By now, everyone in Northwest Cameroon is calling Tantoh "Farmer"—and they say it with pride!

In the Fulani village of Akweto, Tantoh learns that people are drinking from the same stream as their cattle. The water contains harmful bacteria, and many children are getting sick and dying. Tantoh helps the villagers locate a clean spring, but they don't have money for equipment and laborers to build a catchment that can hold the water.

"*Abi yu ngir*," Tantoh says. It is a Limbum phrase for community, meaning "unity is strength." He translates into Fulani so that everyone in the village understands.

Young and old, everyone in Akweto pitches in to clear a path or carry stones. Together, they construct a catchment to capture the spring water. Before long, the entire village has crisp, clean water flowing year-round.

Two years later, a grandfather will tell Farmer Tantoh that since drinking the new water, not one of his neighbors or grandchildren has gotten sick or complained of a stomachache!

One project leads to another and another. Farmer Tantoh founds Save Your Future Association, a nonprofit organization to which people around the world can donate money and supplies. With local and international support, he finds a way to bring clean water to Njirong, a village suffering after a thirty-year conflict.

He begins a water delivery service for blind students. He hires engineers to design stairways, railings, or ramps for villagers with physical disabilities. In places with large populations, communities build reservoirs so that in times of drought, people can get the water they need.

Today, this is northwest Cameroon.

Sometimes wet.

Sometimes dry.

But always very alive.

Today, Farmer Tantoh does not work alone.
A stream of hands works to find fresh,
clean water.
A trickle of hope runs through many villages.
And a crop of young farmers—who are proud
to be farmers—are digging in, planting ideas,
and growing a movement.

AUTHORS' NOTE

In Cameroon, some people preface a tale by saying, "Story long, time short." That's certainly how we have felt while researching and writing this book. In the seven years since we first met Farmer Tantoh Nforba, we've come to discover how wide and deep the impacts of his philosophy and hard work are.

We traveled to northwest Cameroon in 2017, and we were overwhelmed by the number of villagers—from the very young to the elderly—who were beyond eager to tell or show us how Tantoh's work had changed their lives. We visited quite a number of places, including Akweto, Bamenda, Njirong, and Nkambe, his home village. Women danced when they saw Farmer approaching, *fons* (kings or chiefs) invited him into their palaces, and elected officials embraced his work. The highlight, however, was meeting his ninety-year-old grandmother—Sarah Ntala. When we arrived in Taku, her remote village, we found her still working in the gardens that Tantoh loved from the time he was four years old. She dropped to her knees when she saw Farmer. Since she has no phone, electricity, or vehicle, she had no idea her grandson was coming for a visit. Her pride in Farmer was clear, though she still laughs about the stolen onions.

In the twenty years since he first put on the Farmer shirt, Tantoh has installed or consulted on the building of more than sixty wells or spring catchments and inspired the planting of more than eight hundred home, school, or community gardens.

His story is a reminder of many things—being true to your passion, using resources wisely, and never forgetting your roots. Whether you read Farmer Tantoh's story at home or in the classroom, may it inspire you to recognize that one person (even you!) can sow seeds of change and cultivate a brighter future.

—*Baptiste Paul & Miranda Paul*

LIMBUM GLOSSARY AND PRONUNCIATION GUIDE

nshee (nSHEE): dirt or soil

ma kfu (MAHK-foo): grandmother

fufu (FOO-foo): a doughlike dish made from boiled, ground-up corn. In Tantoh's hometown, most fufu is made with corn. However, fufu can also be made from cassava, yam, plantain, or other starchy foods.

abi yu ngir (abee YOU ngeer): community or "unity is strength"

WORDS FOR WATER

In Cameroon, people speak more than 250 languages and dialects. As Farmer Tantoh travels from one village to another, he must learn to communicate with the local people so he can pass on his knowledge and also learn from them. Here are just a few ways to say *water* in various parts of Cameroon.

Language	Word for *Water*	Pronunciation
French	eau	OH
Fulani & Fulfulde	ndiam	DEIM
Limbum	mdiep	MDEEP
Noni	jo	JOE

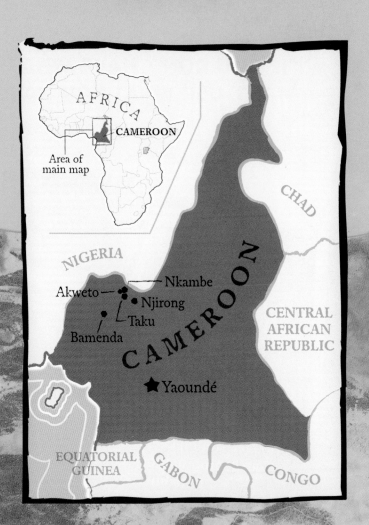

PROVERBS

Proverbs, or wise sayings, are a part of most cultures and languages—especially in the country of Cameroon and on the African continent. Many proverbs are old. Other proverbs are fairly new—in fact, two of the proverbs listed here are Farmer Tantoh originals. These sayings motivate Tantoh and his volunteers while they work together through challenging situations.

"STORY LONG, TIME SHORT."

"YOU ALWAYS LEARN MORE WHEN YOU LOSE THAN WHEN YOU WIN."

"IF YOU DON'T HAVE WHAT YOU WANT, USE WHAT YOU HAVE."*

Farmer Tantoh uses this truck to carry gardening supplies and to deliver water to blind students.

By using the railings that Farmer Tantoh and his volunteers built, villagers can more safely make their way down the mountainside to get the water they need.